Farshore

First published in Great Britain 2021 by Farshore
An imprint of HarperCollins*Publishers*
1 London Bridge Street, London SE1 9GF
www.farshore.co.uk

HarperCollins*Publishers*
1st Floor, Watermarque Building, Ringsend Road
Dublin 4, Ireland

Written by Craig Jelley
Designed by Joe Bolder and Andrea Philpots
Illustrations by Ryan Marsh
Production by Laura Grundy
Special thanks to Sherin Kwan, Alex Wiltshire, Kelsey Howard and Milo Bengtsson

This book is an original creation by Farshore

ISBN 978 0 7555 0042 0
Printed in Italy
007

ONLINE SAFETY FOR YOUNGER FANS

Spending time online is great fun! Here are a few simple rules to help younger fans stay safe and
keep the internet a great place to spend time:
- Never give out your real name – don't use it as your username.
- Never give out any of your personal details.
- Never tell anybody which school you go to or how old you are.
- Never tell anybody your password except a parent or a guardian.
- Be aware that you must be 13 or over to create an account on many sites.
Always check the site policy and ask a parent or guardian for permission before registering.
- Always tell a parent or guardian if something is worrying you.
Stay safe online. Any website addresses listed in this book are correct at the time of going to print.
However, Farshore is not responsible for content hosted by third parties. Please be aware that online
content can be subject to change and websites can contain content that is unsuitable for children.
We advise that all children are supervised when using the internet.

MIX
Paper from
responsible sources
FSC™ C007454

MINECRAFT

COMBAT HANDBOOK

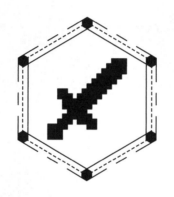

CONTENTS

HELLO

Welcome to the Minecraft Combat Handbook! Survival can be a tricky business. It can feel like something's always out to get you, whether it's your rumbling tummy or a - oh no, is that a Wither skeleton!? No wait, it's just a shadow. A trick of the light ... OR WAS IT?

For any Minecraft adventurer, combat is never far away. Pesky hostile mobs rampage underground as you mine; they emerge at night and bother local friendly villagers; and they positively infest the Nether. And then there's that elite cadre of Minecrafters who live to compete in gladiatorial combat, hearts racing with the clash of netherite!

So no matter how you play, knowing how to fight is a vital skill. You've done the right thing in picking up this book of tactics, advice, information and tricks!

OK, HERE WE GO. HOLD YOUR SWORD TRUE!

BEFORE YOU BEGIN

MODE SELECTION

In the upcoming pages, you'll see tips, tricks and tactics for how to become the bane of any mob or enemy player. You can only fight mobs or other players if your game is in Survival or Adventure modes, and the difficulty isn't set to Peaceful. If you're struggling to get an item you need, you could switch to Creative temporarily and grab it.

MOB ICONS

Throughout this book, you'll meet dozens of mobs, all of which have different stats and drops. Look out for these icons throughout the book.

20

The heart box signifies how many hit points a mob has. The higher it is, the more damage a mob can take.

6

The sword is how much damage a mob can dish out at melee range on normal difficulty, though this can increase on hard.

22.5

The bow signifies how much damage a mob can do from range, again based on normal difficulty.

RECIPES

Where relevant, items are shown with the recipes needed to craft them. Unless otherwise stated, you'll need a crafting table to make them.

The ingredients are the items in the 3x3 grid, and the product is in the lone square beside it.

TOP TIP

Some recipes, like those that show how to craft weapons and tools, will only show one variation. You can use the same recipe above but use different materials to make various kinds of tools and weapons.

Before you launch yourself headlong into a battle with the Ender Dragon brandishing nothing but a wooden hoe, there are some things to explain so that you can make the most out of this book. This spread contains everything you need to know to understand the upcoming pages.

ITEM KEY

arrow of slowness	generated equipment	raw chicken
awkward Potion	ghast tear	raw cod
axe	glass bottle	raw porkchop
blaze powder	glistering melon slice	redstone dust
blaze rod	glowstone dust	rotten flesh
bone	gold nugget	saddle
boots	golden carrot	sand
bow	gunpowder	scute
carrot	helmet	shears
carrot on a stick	hoe	shovel
coal	leggings	shulker shell
cobblestone	music disc	skeleton skull
cooked chicken	nautilus shell	spider eye
creeper head	nether star	stick
crossbow	nether wart	string
chestplate	phantom membrane	sugar
dragon egg	pickaxe	sword
elytra	potato	totem of undying
emerald	potion of fire resistance	trident
enchanted book	potion of healing	tripwire hook
experience points	potion of swiftness	turtle shell
feather	potion of water breathing	warped fungus on a stick
fermented spider eye	prismarine crystals	water bottle
fishing rod	prismarine shard	wet sponge
flint	pufferfish	wither skeleton skull
flint and steel	rabbit's foot	zombie head

BE PREPARED

A wise adventurer is always prepared before they
step on the battlefield. Of course, this means ensuring
you've got the best weapons and armour, but that's
just the tip of the arrow. Explore with us the myriad
choices at your fingertips to turn you into a feared
warrior, from swords and shields to foods,
potions and enchantments.

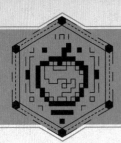

MAKING SENSE OF THE SCREEN

1 HOTBAR
This bar is like a mini-inventory that you can populate with your favourite items, weapons and tools to make it easy to switch between them.

2 SELECTED ITEM
You can tell the item you have selected by the thick box around the icon. If a weapon or tool is selected, pressing the Use button will swing it.

3 OFFHAND SLOT
The offhand slot allows you to select a secondary item to take into battle – shields can be equipped here, as well as different types of arrows.

4 HEALTH
Hearts signify how much health you have – each is worth two points. As you take damage, the hearts will disappear. If they all go, it's game over!

TOP TIP
You can customise the blocks that appear in your hotbar by accessing the inventory screen. The hotbar is the bottom row of the inventory screen and you can drag your owned items from the inventory to your hotbar so that you can easily access them rather than navigating back to the inventory screen.

The first thing you'll want to do ahead of entering combat is make sure that you know what you're looking at. The heads-up display (HUD) shows you everything you need to know at a glance, from your health and hunger to the weapons you're wielding.

5 ARMOUR

If you have at least one piece of armour, you'll see chestplates appear. These icons work the same as the health hearts – 2 armour points per chestplate icon. Every armour point blocks 4% of incoming damage.

6 HUNGER

These drumsticks signify how hungry you are – one represents 2 hunger points. It doesn't need to be full, but if it's empty, you'll take damage until you eat again. If your hunger is less than 3, you'll also be unable to run.

7 OXYGEN

When you dive underwater, you'll have a limited supply of oxygen to keep you going. It'll reset if you resurface or get air in a bubble column, but if it runs out, you'll begin to periodically take damage and drown.

8 EXPERIENCE POINTS

Whenever you mine ores, hook a fish with a rod, defeat a mob or complete many other actions, you'll receive green experience orbs that will raise your level. You can then use your levels on unlocking enchantments!

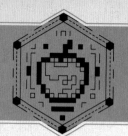

CHOOSE YOUR WEAPON

SWORD

TYPES						
ATTACK STRENGTH	5	6	7	5	8	9
DURABILITY	60	132	251	33	1562	2032

The trusty sword is probably the first weapon you used in Minecraft, and there's likely been one by your side ever since. Of course, it was made for battle so does more damage than most tools, is enchantable and attacks faster than most alternatives.

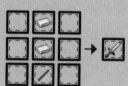

TRIDENT

TYPES	
ATTACK STRENGTH	8-9
DURABILITY	251

Obtainable only from a drowned, the trident is a versatile weapon that can be used at melee and ranged distances. Tridents can receive special enchantments that either make it return after a throw, pin an enemy in place, or call lightning down from the sky!

TOP TIP

It's important to consider a weapon's speed as well. Swords do more damage than an axe, and are quicker to swing, meaning you can do much more damage with a sword.

It wouldn't be combat if you weren't armed to the teeth with an arsenal of powerful weapons. You might think you're sorted once you've got your hands on a sword, but there are also some items and blocks you can call upon that you might not have been expecting.

BOW AND ARROW

TYPES	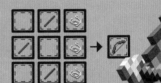
ATTACK STRENGTH	1-10
DURABILITY	384

The trusty bow is an entry-level ranged weapon that fires arrows. The damage they rain down depends on how long you charge each shot for – the longer you charge, the more pain it will cause an enemy. You can craft a bow from sticks and string, and arrows from a stick, a feather and a piece of flint.

CROSSBOW

TYPES	
ATTACK STRENGTH	9
DURABILITY	464

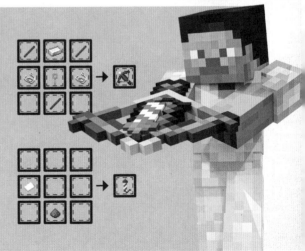

The crossbow can do everything a bow can do, but a little bit slower and more powerfully too. However, it has one very clever trick – it can also shoot firework rockets! If the firework has been crafted with a firework star, it will cause additional explosive damage! Up to 7 firework stars can be used to create a firework and increase damage.

AXE

TYPES						
ATTACK STRENGTH	4	5	6	4	7	8
DURABILITY	60	132	251	33	1562	2032

Commonly used to chop trees, the axe is a deadly weapon too – only slightly less powerful than a sword, though much slower. The gold axe has poor strength and durability, but if you can spare the materials, the netherite one can float on lava.

HOE, SHOVEL AND PICKAXE

TYPES						
ATTACK STRENGTH	1	2	2	2	3	3
DURABILITY	55	165	165	77	363	407

If you're caught short and don't have a traditional weapon to hand, you can wield one of your many tools instead. They're weaker than swords and axes, and also consume two durability points per hit – as an axe does too – so most of them won't last you very long. Still, the diamond and netherite versions can cause a decent amount of damage, and they're stronger than using your fists!

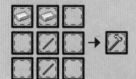 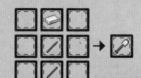 

TNT

TYPES	
ATTACK STRENGTH	N/A
DURABILITY	N/A

Now we're getting to the good stuff! TNT is an explosive block that can be triggered to detonate after a short delay. It will destroy blocks in a blast radius and cause damage and knockback to any mobs in the vicinity – the more TNT used, the bigger the explosion. Mobs that are closer to the TNT will take more damage. It can be hooked up to redstone so that it's possible to activate from a safe distance.

SNOWBALL

TYPES	
ATTACK STRENGTH	0
DURABILITY	N/A

You can find snowballs by destroying snow blocks and snow layers. They're more of an annoyance than a weapon as they don't cause any damage, but instead knock a player or mob back – perfect for trying to push mobs off cliff edges. The only mob that they can damage is the blaze, which seems to have a particular aversion to being doused by the cold snow.

EGG

TYPES	
ATTACK STRENGTH	0
DURABILITY	N/A

Like snowballs, the egg is a non-damaging projectile that pushes mobs and players. They're collected from farms, so you should be able to head into battle with plenty to hand. Sometimes when you throw an egg, a chicken will hatch, so it could also distract enemy players for a while ...

FIRE CHARGE

TYPES	
ATTACK STRENGTH	5-9
DURABILITY	N/A

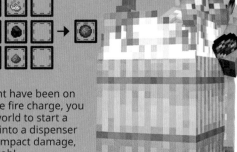

If you've taken a trip to the Nether, you might have been on the receiving end of a fireball or ten. With the fire charge, you can turn the tables. Use it anywhere in the world to start a fire, just like a flint and steel does, or load it into a dispenser to shoot a fireball straight ahead. It'll cause impact damage, and also start a fire when it hits a block or mob!

DISPENSER

TYPES	
ATTACK STRENGTH	N/A
DURABILITY	N/A

Take the manual labour out of ranged attacks by placing a dispenser to do your launching activities for you. As well as shooting fire charges, the dispenser can also launch arrows, splash and lingering potions, eggs and snowballs, firework rockets, lava buckets and even a trident. Combine a dispenser with levers, pressure plates or another redstone mechanism to automate your attack and set defensive traps.

LAVA BUCKET

TYPES	
ATTACK STRENGTH	N/A
DURABILITY	N/A

Consider using a lava bucket as your last resort if a battle is going badly. You can fill a bucket by using it on any lava source. Using the bucket will create a lava source block, causing lava flows around an area and scorching the earth under your feet. It will cause damage to many mobs every couple of seconds but render the battlefield unusable. Probably better to use from high ground ...

ARMOUR & ELYTRA

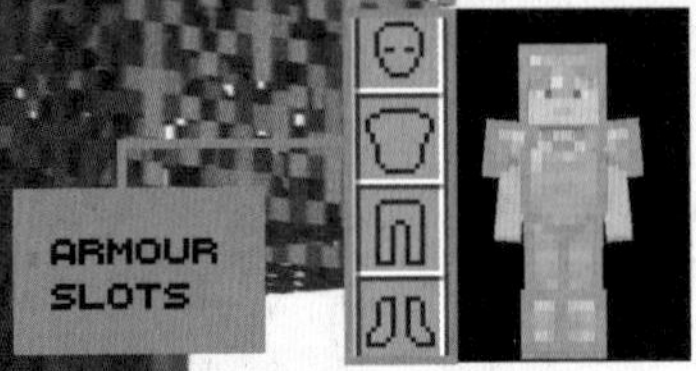

ARMOUR SLOTS

HELMET

TURTLE SHELL

Crafted from scutes dropped by baby turtles, the turtle shell is a unique helmet that triggers the Water Breathing effect when submerged. It's durability is second only to diamond and netherite helms, and offers the same defence as iron and gold variants.

ELYTRA

Found in loot stashes in End ships, elytra aren't really armour as they offer no protection, but they occupy the same slot as a chestplate. They're great for springing surprise aerial attacks or making a swift retreat.

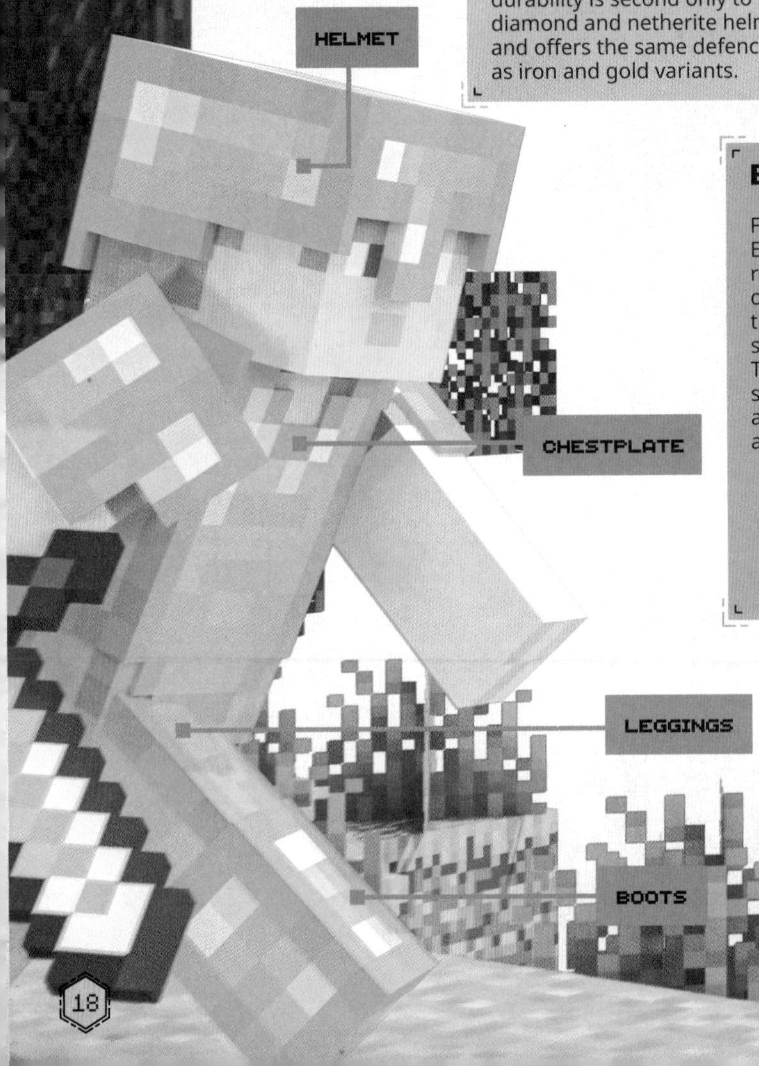

CHESTPLATE

LEGGINGS

BOOTS

Every warrior will take damage, but you can lessen the impact by putting on armour before you charge into battle. Every piece you wear gives you an amount of armour points, which appear above your health, and you can even enchant armour for additional protection.

HELMET

TYPES						
ARMOUR POINTS	1	2	2	2	3	3
DURABILITY	55	165	165	77	363	407

Helmets fit into the head slot, and offer a little armour. They can take Protection enchantments, as well as helmet-specific ones such as Aqua Affinity, which increases mining rate while in water.

CHESTPLATE

TYPES						
ARMOUR POINTS	3	5	6	5	8	8
DURABILITY	80	240	240	112	528	592

Chestplates offer more armour points than any item. They're worn in the torso slot and can be enchanted with any of the Protection spells, as well as Thorns, which can inflict some damage back at foes.

LEGGINGS

TYPES						
ARMOUR POINTS	2	4	5	3	6	6
DURABILITY	75	225	225	105	495	555

In the lower-body slot, you can equip leggings. They're second only to chestplates in the armour they allow. There are no specific legging enchantments but Unbreaking boosts their great durability.

BOOTS

TYPES						
ARMOUR POINTS	1	1	2	1	3	3
DURABILITY	65	195	195	91	429	481

Boots don't offer huge protection, but they do have a few useful enchantments such as Depth Strider, which increases speed underwater, and Feather Falling, which minimises fall damage.

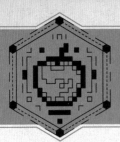

HEALTH AND HUNGER

HEALTH EFFECTS

When you spawn in any world, you'll have 10 drumsticks on your hunger bar, which equal 20 hunger points. As you perform actions – breaking blocks, attacking mobs, running, jumping, swimming – your hunger bar will shrink. The varying levels of your hunger will have different effects.

If hunger level is at 18 or above, you'll gradually regain lost health points.

When your hunger drops below 18 points, you'll neither lose nor regain health.

As the hunger bar hits 0, you'll begin to lose a health point every few seconds.

When hunger is at or below 6 points, you'll lose the ability to sprint!

When hunger is above 18 points, you'll get an instant heal of 2 health points when you take any form of damage.

We've seen how you can protect your head, feet and other body parts with armour, but how about protecting your belly? Hunger is affected by every action you do, and can have a massive effect on your health and abilities, so it's in a warrior's best interest to keep their stomach sated.

TASTY TREATS

You can refill your hunger bar with food. Thankfully, you can find it pretty much everywhere you turn in Minecraft, from simple crops to hearty soups. Here are the treats you can use to replenish different amounts of hunger points:

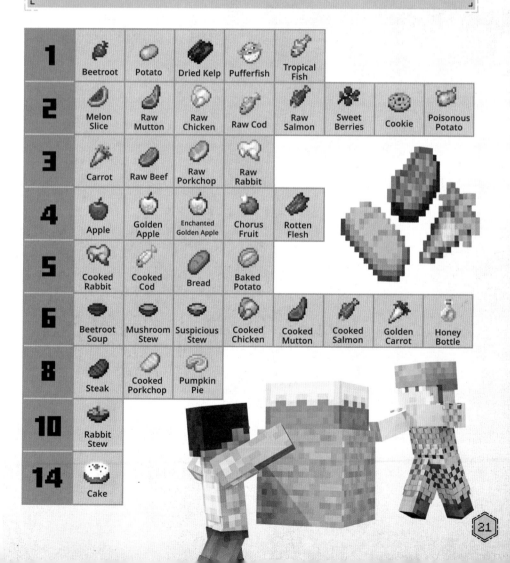

1 — Beetroot | Potato | Dried Kelp | Pufferfish | Tropical Fish

2 — Melon Slice | Raw Mutton | Raw Chicken | Raw Cod | Raw Salmon | Sweet Berries | Cookie | Poisonous Potato

3 — Carrot | Raw Beef | Raw Porkchop | Raw Rabbit

4 — Apple | Golden Apple | Enchanted Golden Apple | Chorus Fruit | Rotten Flesh

5 — Cooked Rabbit | Cooked Cod | Bread | Baked Potato

6 — Beetroot Soup | Mushroom Stew | Suspicious Stew | Cooked Chicken | Cooked Mutton | Cooked Salmon | Golden Carrot | Honey Bottle

8 — Steak | Cooked Porkchop | Pumpkin Pie

10 — Rabbit Stew

14 — Cake

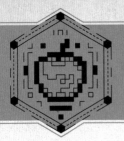

DIMENSION HOPPING

THE NETHER

HOW TO GET THERE

The Nether is the easiest of the two dimensions to reach. You can create a portal in the Overworld using obsidian to make a rectangular frame, anywhere between 4 x 5 blocks and 23 x 23. Once the frame has been completed, light it with a flint and steel and a purple portal will appear before you.

LANDSCAPE

The Nether has several varied biomes – each of them is dimly lit and prone to lavafalls or random fire. They range from the alien vegetations of the crimson and warped forests, to the flammable Nether wastes. You'll also spot a few structures, like ruined portals and bastion remnants throughout.

DENIZENS

The mobs that roam the Nether are largely hostile beasts – blazes, magma cubes and ghasts are a few examples. A couple of them have fiery attacks, while piglins can actually be quite friendly ... if you're dressed in gold. A couple of Overworld mobs, like the Enderman and skeleton, seem to have accidentally wandered through a portal too.

It's never too early to think about taking a trip away from the Overworld into the Nether and End dimensions. Visiting these dangerous realms is a necessity if you want to get your hands on the best equipment and items. Brace yourself for a perilous journey ...

THE END

HOW TO GET THERE

Reaching the End means finding a stronghold, which holds an incomplete End portal made of End portal blocks. Before you can activate the portal, all the blocks need to have eyes of Ender placed in them. The eyes of Ender are crafted with blaze powder and Ender pearls that are dropped by Endermen.

LANDSCAPE

Its inky sky is pierced by pale yellow End stone and violet purpur bricks that make up the dimension. When you first enter the End, a cluster of islands will lead to the Ender Dragon, but once you've vanquished it, you'll have access to the End city, where ships float above exotic chorus trees.

DENIZENS

There aren't too many mobs that call the End their home, but the ones that do can be quite a handful. Of course, the Ender Dragon will cause the most problems for you, but the shulker's Levitation effect is more annoying than most attacks. And of course, the Enderman has made it here too. Is there anywhere it can't go?

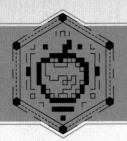

DIMENSION SHOPPING LIST

BLAZE ROD / BLAZE POWDER

If you plan on doing any brewing, you'll need to get at least one blaze rod, which is used in the recipe for a brewing stand. Blazes, which you'll find in Nether fortresses, have a chance to drop a blaze rod on defeat. You can grind them up into blaze powder, which is used in the brewing process.

DRAGON'S BREATH

This is probably going to be the most difficult item to get as you'll need to face the Ender Dragon. Scoop up either the dragon's breath attack or fireball into an empty glass bottle and you'll be able to combine it with any potion to turn it into a lingering variant.

GLOWSTONE DUST

You'll notice the Nether's dark environment is lit by clusters of glowstone. Mine these blocks and you'll receive up to 4 pieces of glowstone dust, used in brewing to make the effects of a potion stronger. It can also be used to craft firework stars, which can help to make explosive crossbow ammo.

NETHER WART

Take a trip to the Nether fortress or bastion remnant biomes of the Nether and you might find crops of Nether wart lying around, which you can harvest for up to 4 Nether warts each. They're imperative in brewing as they're used to create Awkward Potions – the base ingredient for most of the potions you'll need to brew!

MAGMA CREAM

Defeating all but the smallest variety of magma cube will give you the chance to pick up some magma cream, which will allow you to brew a Potion of Fire Resistance. Such a potion will come in handy when fighting many of the fiery Nether folk.

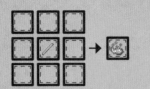

Now you've found your way to these strange dimensions and briefly met some of their inhabitants, you might be wondering what you should be looking out for. This handy guide will give you a list of items that you can use to make some super-useful items to aid you in combat.

ANCIENT DEBRIS

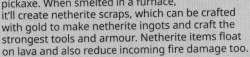

One of the rarest ore blocks in Minecraft, ancient debris is found solely in the Nether and can only be mined with a diamond or netherite pickaxe. When smelted in a furnace, it'll create netherite scraps, which can be crafted with gold to make netherite ingots and craft the strongest tools and armour. Netherite items float on lava and also reduce incoming fire damage too.

ELYTRA

Once you've taken down the Ender Dragon, you'll have a chance to visit the End city, a biome of the End protected by sneaky shulkers. If you make your way to one of the giant End ships floating in the biome, you should find a loot chest containing an elytra, which will give you the power to glide when worn.

GHAST TEAR

If you can survive a barrage of fireballs from a ghast and manage to defeat it, you may be able to get your hands on a ghast tear. You can find ghasts in the basalt delta, soul sand valley and Nether waste biomes of the Nether. Ghast tears can be used to brew Potions of Regeneration, which top up your health every few seconds.

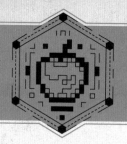

ENCHANTING WORKFLOW

WHAT CAN I ENCHANT?

First of all, you'll need an enchanting table, which is made with a book, diamonds and obsidian blocks. The enchanting table will allow you to weave your powerful magic into armour, weapons and other items like pickaxes, shears and fishing rods.

USING AN ENCHANTING TABLE

When you interact with an enchanting table, you'll see this window appear – the enchanting interface.

Place the item that you want to enchant in this slot

This box will display up to 3 random enchantments that you can apply to the item

Here is where you'll place the required amount of lapis lazuli – 1 to 3 pieces

The number on the left is how many experience levels you'll use to imbue the item with this enchantment

This is the enchantment level, which indicates how powerful it will be

The enchantments you see are random, and based on the item you want to enchant, how many lapis lazuli you've placed, and the number of surrounding bookshelves. The enchantments are written in the standard galactic alphabet, but if you hover over them, you'll get a hint to what enchantment you're about to choose.

No matter what weapons you have to hand, they can always be made more powerful on an enchanting table. Enchanting is a process that exchanges your experience points and lapis lazuli for additional abilities or increased stats on items.

UNLOCK POWERFUL ENCHANTMENTS

To access the most powerful level of enchantments, you'll need vast knowledge ... or books that contain it anyway. An enchanting table will draw power from nearby bookshelves to unlock its full potential. You'll see alien glyphs floating into the enchanting table from bookshelves a block away.

The optimum number of bookshelves that you need to unlock the most powerful enchantments is 15. The bookshelves should each be a block-space away from the enchanting table, but can also be a space higher as well. Here's an example library that you can copy.

CURSES

On your adventures, you might find a couple of items that have bad enchantments on them – curses. The Curse of Binding prevents an armour being removed, yet the Curse of Vanishing will make an item disappear if you die.

TOP TIP

Turn the page to discover which enchantments you can bestow on different items.

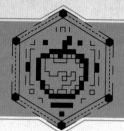

EXCITING ENCHANTMENTS

MELEE

BANE OF ARTHROPODS

Increases the damage you'll do to insectoid mobs.

FIRE ASPECT

Sets a target on fire when a strike lands.

LOOTING

Increases the chance of mobs dropping loot.

KNOCKBACK

Adds more knockback to standard attacks.

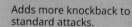

ARMOUR

FEATHER FALLING

Decreases fall damage that is taken.

BLAST PROTECTION

Additional defence against explosions.

FIRE PROTECTION

Reduces damage from fire, decreases burn time.

PROJECTILE PROTECTION

Additional defence against projectiles like arrows.

PROTECTION

Decreases all damage types slightly.

Now you know how to enchant, there's just one question left to answer: what should I enchant? These pages show all the most useful enchantments that you can bestow on your equipment to aid you in your battles. Pick your favourites and get to work!

RANGED

INFINITY

Prevents the expenditure of normal arrows.

FLAME

Sets a target on fire with an arrow.

POWER

Every arrow you shoot causes much more damage.

MULTISHOT

Fires 3 arrows but only expends one.

TRIDENT

LOYALTY

Returns the trident to you after it stops.

CHANNELLING

Calls lightning from the sky to strike mobs hit by a trident.

RIPTIDE

Player travels with a thrown trident when in water or rain.

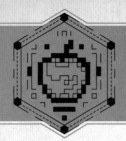

SOMETHING'S BREWING ...

WHAT DO I NEED?

The first thing you'll need to get your hands on is a brewing stand. You can find these in village churches, igloos and end ships, or craft them with a blaze rod and 3 blocks of cobblestone or blackstone. You'll also need:

Glass bottles are the base of potions.

Blaze powder fuels the brewing and can craft 20 potions per piece.

Cauldrons can be used to fill bottles with water, though any source will do.

Other items will add the different effects to your potions.

BREWING STAND GUI

When you interact with a brewing stand, it will bring up the brewing interface.

This slot is for blaze powder – it will glow and fill up the bubbles if it's creating a new potion.

This slot is for the ingredient you want to add – it will feed into the three bottles and change the water or potion in the bottle slots.

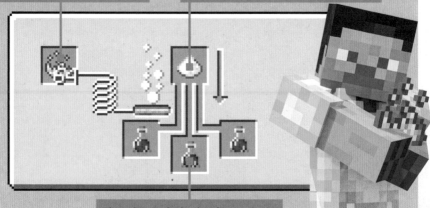

These slots are for bottles of water or potions. Up to three can be added at once.

Enchantments can offer you protection and boost your abilities, but they're not the only way to achieve such results. Brewing will allow you to concoct a variety of potions that can give you an edge in battle, or alternatively cause mayhem for your poor opponents.

BREWING 101

1 First of all, fill your bottles up with water from a cauldron or natural water source.

2 Place the bottles of water in the three slots and load up some blaze powder into the fuel.

3 Before you add an effect to a potion, you need to make a base, so add some nether wart to the ingredient slot to create three awkward potions. Awkward potions are the base for the majority of potions.

4 Now finally we can add an effect ingredient. Leave the awkward potions where they are and add some sugar. Wait a little while and those awkward potions will become potions of swiftness.

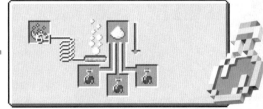

5 Now take the potions out of the bottle slots and put them in your inventory, ready to gulp when you need them.

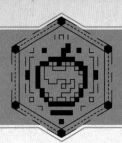

POTENT POTIONS

POTION OF FIRE RESISTANCE

Grants immunity to fire, lava, magma and some fireballs.

POTION OF STRENGTH

Increases the power of your melee attacks, armed and unarmed.

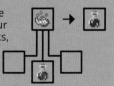

POTION OF WEAKNESS

Reduces melee attack power. Uses a water bottle, not Awkward Potion.

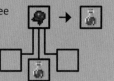

POTION OF NIGHT VISION

Lets you see in the dark almost as clearly as in bright daylight.

POTION OF SLOW FALLING

Makes players fall gently and prevents any falling damage.

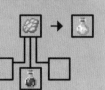

POTION OF THE TURTLE MASTER

Makes a player move slower, but take less damage.

POTION OF WATER BREATHING

Lets the player stay underwater for the duration.

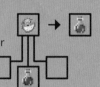

POTION OF REGENERATION

Restores health gradually over a short period of time.

What noxious liquids will you decide to cook up next? Will they heal or harm, float or fall? Have a look at this list of useful concoctions and see which ones take your fancy. Most potions use an Awkward Potion as their base, unless it says otherwise. Refer to the item key on page 7 if you get stuck.

POTION OF LEAPING

Allows players to jump to a greater height for a short period of time.

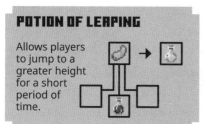

POTION OF SWIFTNESS

Enables players to move much faster and see more of the world around.

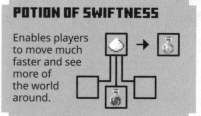

POTION OF SLOWNESS

Reduces the movement speed of an enemy.

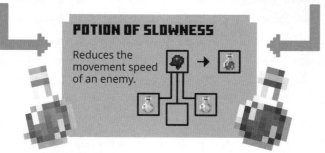

POTION OF HEALING

Instantly replenishes a small amount of health.

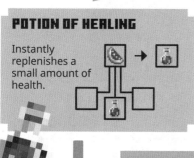

POTION OF POISON

Causes gradual health loss over a short period of time.

POTION OF HARMING

Causes an instant amount of damage to enemies.

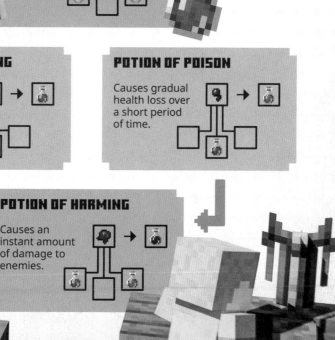

KNOW YOUR ENEMY

Only fools in damaged leather armour rush straight into battle. Smarter warriors will take some time to learn the strengths and weaknesses of their enemies so they can best them in mortal combat. The following pages shine a torch on all the mobs that await you in Minecraft, from the slippery silverfish to the epic Ender Dragon. But they're not all bad – some will even help you out!

BLAZE

Hot-headed flying mob fuelled by anger	♥	⚔	🏹	
	20	6	5	

Drops

✏ ⬡ 10 XP

Blazes are native to Nether fortresses and will chase down any player within a 48-block radius. They will also call in allies as back-up when they're attempting to ambush an unlucky target. They can fly and will often swarm with their buddies and try to attack a player from above.

When a blaze has a player in its sights, it will launch up to three fireballs, which do five points of damage each. If they miss their target, they'll create fire wherever they hit. Blazes can also cause significant damage if you touch their fiery exterior! They take damage from fire-dousing items such as water and snowballs, though you can defeat them by more traditional means too.

HOW TO DEFEAT

As the old saying goes, it's best to fight fire with ... snow? Shields are the only defence against a blaze's fireball, so make sure to have one in your offhand slot to block its attacks, then pelt it with snowballs, which cause three points of damage each as they fizzle on the blaze's fire.

CHICKEN JOCKEY

Bizarre combo of farm bird and infant flesh-eater	20/4	⚔️ 3	🏹 N/A

Drops

22 -25 XP

When baby variants of zombies, zombie villagers, husks and zombified piglins attempt to spawn, there's a 5% chance it will spawn as a chicken jockey if there's a suitable chicken in the area.

The baby zombie (and its variants) share stats with their adult counterparts and often spawn with equipment, making it more dangerous. Baby zombified piglins riding a chicken can be three times stronger than normal baby zombies!

HOW TO DEFEAT

Save the chicken by using a bucket of water on the jockey, which will separate the mob combo and allow the chicken to escape. Then unleash a barrage of speedy sword attacks to defeat the baby zombie that's left – ranged weapons are harder because the babies are so fast!

CREEPER

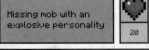

Hissing mob with an
explosive personality

20   0   43

Drops

5 XP

Creepers move silently across the Overworld.
The first thing you'll hear is their hiss as
they prepare to detonate. Their explosion
has a blast radius of 7 blocks, but players
can run when they hear the hiss to halt the
detonation, or block the blast with a shield.

Very rarely, you might see a creeper that
has been struck by lightning, known as a
charged creeper. It will be cloaked in blue
electricity and its explosive power is amped
up considerably – when a charged creeper
explodes, it's even more powerful than TNT!

HOW TO DEFEAT

Keep your distance! The creeper can't blow up in your face if your face is
several blocks away. Attack with a crossbow to deal the most ranged damage
with better accuracy than a bow and keep circling away from it with every shot.

DROWNED

Soggy undead dweller of the seas	20	11	9

Drops
     5-12 XP

Drowned naturally spawn underwater or as a result of a normal zombie drowning – hence the name. They're aggressive to players, baby turtles, villagers and wandering traders and will hunt them down out of water.

During the day they will stay at the bottom of water bodies and chase swimming entities – they can swim at the same speed as a player. At night, they emerge to seek their prey. Baby drowned drop more XP.

HOW TO DEFEAT

They're harder to defeat underwater, so wait until night, when they emerge to seek flesh. Stay away so they resort to ranged attacks. Try to dodge, especially if they throw a trident, as it's very powerful – then pelt them with arrows from a bow. Once defeated, you might have a chance to take their trident!

ELDER GUARDIAN

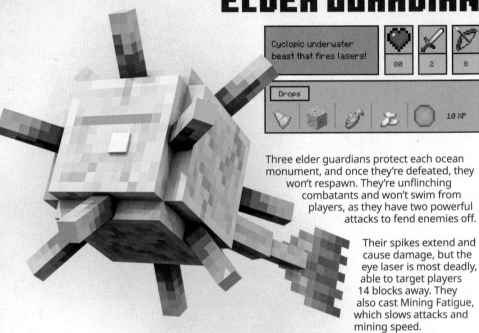

Cyclopic underwater beast that fires lasers!

❤️ 80
🗡️ 2
🏹 8

Drops

10 XP

Three elder guardians protect each ocean monument, and once they're defeated, they won't respawn. They're unflinching combatants and won't swim from players, as they have two powerful attacks to fend enemies off.

Their spikes extend and cause damage, but the eye laser is most deadly, able to target players 14 blocks away. They also cast Mining Fatigue, which slows attacks and mining speed.

HOW TO DEFEAT

The elder guardian is most deadly when it's targeting you with its laser, so make sure to hide behind cover if you see the beam charging. It's susceptible to the Impaling enchantment, which boosts the attack power of tridents. Launch an Impaling-enchanted trident at the elder guardian, dodge and hide — if the trident is also enchanted with Loyalty, you can summon it back and repeat the process.

ENDERMITE

Insect annoyance that appear as if by magic	8	2	N/A

Drops				
			◯	3 XP

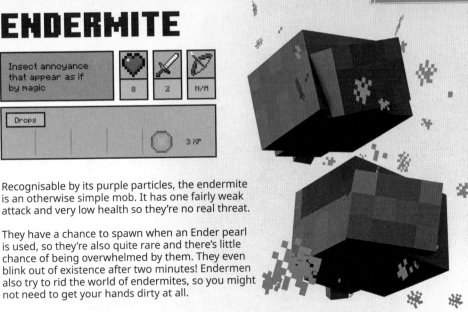

Recognisable by its purple particles, the endermite is an otherwise simple mob. It has one fairly weak attack and very low health so they're no real threat.

They have a chance to spawn when an Ender pearl is used, so they're also quite rare and there's little chance of being overwhelmed by them. They even blink out of existence after two minutes! Endermen also try to rid the world of endermites, so you might not need to get your hands dirty at all.

HOW TO DEFEAT

You need not waste too much time against the endermite. Their relatively low health means that you can dispatch one of them with a single blow from a stone axe. In fact, if you enchant even a wooden axe with the Bane Of Arthropods enchantment – which causes more damage to insect mobs – you can use that to one-hit endermites too!

EVOKER

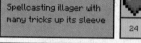

Spellcasting illager with many tricks up its sleeve

 24   N/A   6

Drops

10 XP

A master of magics found in woodland mansions and raids. It raises its arms to cast a spell: when purple particles appear, gnashing fangs emerge from the ground. When the particles are white, it summons a vex to help.

HOW TO DEFEAT

The cooldown of each of the evoker's offensive spells is at least 5 seconds – longer if it tries to cast the same one twice in a row – so if you can nimbly dodge the fangs, dart in with a sword, slash a couple of times and get a safe distance away. Repeat until the evoker is vanquished.

VEX

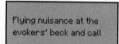

Flying nuisance at the evokers' beck and call

 14   9   N/A

Drops

 5 XP

Summoned only by an evoker, they attack on command with an iron sword. For small mobs, they pack a punch – each strike is stronger than their master's attacks! They can also pass through blocks to avoid retaliation, making them very … vexing.

HOW TO DEFEAT

Vexes are agile beasts that often float out of reach. They glow red when they are about to attack, so you could smash a lingering Potion of Harming on the ground before they swoop in, or poke them with the long trident. They will take damage a few minutes after spawning though, so focus on the evoker first.

GHAST

Floating menace with a fierce fireball attack	10	N/A	12

Drops

  5 XP

Doomed to endlessly roam the Nether, the ghast's huge, haunting visage is a common sight in the hellish dimension. It has very low health, but a deadly fireball attack to compensate.

It shoots a fireball at any visible player within 64 blocks, and will continue to fire every few seconds until it's defeated or out of sight. The fireballs travel relatively slowly and are easily dodged, but travel infinitely in a straight line. If you're unlucky enough to let one hit you, it will cause explosive damage and light nearby netherrack.

HOW TO DEFEAT

The ghast has a big weakness: its own fireballs. Strike one with a melee weapon or projectile to return it to sender. If it hits the ghast, it does 1000 points of damage. If this sounds risky, a bow and some patient shooting will do the job too.

GUARDIAN

Lesser underwater cyclopic beast ... still deadly			
	30	2	6

Drops

 | | | | 10 XP

The smaller sibling of the elder guardian, the guardian shares many characteristics with its counterpart. It also has a spiky attack and a laser that it can shoot out of its single eye, which causes a similar amount of damage, though each guardian has considerably lower health than the elder variant.

But what it lacks in health, the guardian makes up for in brains – unlike its elder brethren, the guardian will swim away from players and make evasive manoeuvres so it can attack from a distance with its deadlier laser attack.

HOW TO DEFEAT

Guardians are also susceptible to an Impaling-enchanted trident, but as they're more defensively minded, it might be better to try for a melee barrage than a ranged trident offensive. Be sure to place a few blocks for cover as you chase them down.

HOGLIN

Nether native with a vicious charge attack			
	40	8	N/A

 Drops

3 XP

You might find this beast wandering the crimson forests of the Nether. They charge at players in the vicinity and fling them in the air like ragdolls. They have an aversion to some blocks, like warped fungi and Nether portals and will avoid these if possible.

HOW TO DEFEAT

Use a hoglin's fear against it – stand in a plot of warped fungi to keep the hoglin interested but too scared to approach and launch arrows at it from a safe distance. Make sure the plot is at least 4x4 or it might still choose to ignore its fears and attack you anyway. Baby hoglins, understandably, do less damage.

ZOGLIN

A zombified transplant from the Nether			
	40	8	N/A

 Drops

3 XP

When portal-averse hoglins enter the Overworld, they undergo a hideous transformation into a zombified variant. In zoglin form, they shed fears of certain blocks, though retain the powerful charge attack.

HOW TO DEFEAT

As an undead mob, the zoglin takes damage from items that give Instant Health. If you can maintain distance and pelt it with splash Potions of Healing, you can make light work of one. If you do end up taking any damage from being thrown, you'll already have an item on hand to top up your health too.

HUSK

Desert-flavoured zombies immune to sunlight			
	20	3	N/A

Drops   3 XP

Confined to the barren sands of desert biomes, the husk is a more resilient variant of the zombie that suffers no damage from exposure to daylight.

They pursue players from a greater distance than zombies – up to 40 blocks away – and inflict Hunger on any player they hit, which depletes the player's hunger level more quickly. They often spawn with a variety of equipment too, but thankfully nothing more dangerous than an iron sword.

HOW TO DEFEAT

Husks don't really have a clear weakness to exploit, so the good old shield-and-sword combo should do just the trick! Blocking any attacks with a shield will prevent the Hunger status effect, and a decent sword should make light work of even a well-armoured husk.

MAGMA CUBE

Combustible creature that comes in three hot sizes			
	1/4/16	3/4/6	N/A

Drops				
				1-4 XP

Isn't it frightening when you think you've defeated an enemy, only for them to split into many smaller versions? The magma cube is such a mob – the large one splits into 2-4 medium cubes when vanquished, which in turn split into 2-4 small versions.

They can only damage you by contact, but they're twice as fast as most other mobs and often spring up in the air in an attempt to squish you when they land. Luckily, they only reside in the Nether.

HOW TO DEFEAT

Magma cubes are resistant to fall and fire damages, as well as being fast and unpredictable. It can't damage you if it can't land on you, so build yourself a little den with a single block gap in each wall and the roof. Ready your bow and take shots at it whenever it tries to jump on you.

PHANTOM

Winged stalker of the sleepless

❤	⚔	🏹
20	6	N/A

Drops

5 XP

Sleep is a necessity for any warrior – it rejuvenates health, gives you bizarre dreams and stops the horrific phantom descending on you. Yes, the phantom will appear only at night when you have gone without sleep for three consecutive in-game days!

Groups of up to four phantoms will spawn at once, circling the sky, and attempt to swoop down to attack at regular intervals. The phantom's health is equivalent to a common zombie, but its attack is almost three times as vicious, so a pack of them can be tricky to deal with.

HOW TO DEFEAT

Phantoms take damage like other undead creatures. Enchanting a sword with Smite will increase the damage it causes to a phantom, and you should time your attacks for when it swoops. It also takes damage from sunlight, so you could wait until morning and it'll disappear. Maybe just get some sleep next time!

PIGLIN

Porcine people with a penchant for gold

| 16 | 9 | 4 |

Drops

 5-17 XP

Some assume the piglin to be passive – they must have been wearing golden armour, which piglins love. Without golden armour, the piglin is very hostile and can cause great damage with its melee attack. They also hate ores being mined and chests opening.

HOW TO DEFEAT

Piglins like gold, but how about iron? Test the theory by building an iron golem. The piglin won't immediately attack the golem, presumably as it decides whether it likes this metal too, but the golem will attack the piglin. Make sure you're wearing gold armour while you're building otherwise the piglin will attack you anyway.

ZOMBIFIED PIGLIN

Pigfolk of the Nether raised from the dead

| 20 | 8 | 4 |

Drops

5-12 XP

These zombie-style piglins spawn in the Nether, or are created when a piglin or piglin brute enters another dimension, or when a pig is hit by lightning! They're neutral until harmed and will attack with a gold sword!

HOW TO DEFEAT

Smite works as well on a zombified piglin as other undead, however, this mob has a knack for calling in its brethren within a huge radius. The best mode of attack is to not engage at all – load a dispenser with splash Potions of Healing and a pressure plate in front of it so it can be the architect of its own downfall!

PIGLIN BRUTE

A porked-up version
of the piglin

| 50 | 10 | N/A |

Drops

  20 XP

As if the piglin wasn't enough of a hassle, some of them have been pumping iron ore and turned into brutes. Luckily they confine themselves to bastion remnant structures, although they can often be found swinging an enchanted golden axe, so it's not all good news.

They have a more powerful attack than a piglin and can take more damage before they're defeated. Like piglins, they will attack Withers and Wither skeletons on sight, but they're not as enthralled by gold items as their non-brute counterparts.

HOW TO DEFEAT

The saying goes that the enemy of an enemy is a friend, so make a friend of the piglin brutes by summoning a Wither and pit the mobs against each other. Best case scenario, they decimate each other and leave you with a killing blow to make. Worst case ... well ... turn to page 60 if you need help.

PILLAGER

Crossbow-wielding raid terror			
	24	3	4

Drops

     5-20 XP

Found in outposts or raiding villages, pillagers are a menace. They target innocents with crossbows and pursue from up to 64 blocks away! They may also inflict the Bad Omen effect if they're a captain, which will summon a raid to the next village an afflicted player enters.

HOW TO DEFEAT

Pillagers are good crossbow users, but you can do better. Load your crossbow with firework rockets to give an explosive retort to their bolts! Every firework star you use to create the firework rocket increases the damage a little bit too, so you can cause up to 18 damage with a single well-placed rocket.

RAVAGER

Colossal charging steed of war			
	100	12	6

Drops

 20 XP

Often ridden by illagers, ravagers are a dangerous mob in their own right. They spawn only in raids, and ram players, villagers and other friendly folk in charging attacks, trampling any crops in their way. They have an immense amount of health.

HOW TO DEFEAT

It might defy logic, but you can block a ravager's charge with a shield, nullifying damage and reducing knockback. This may also stun the ravager, allowing you to slash at it before it comes to. When it does react, it will release a damaging roar, so make sure you don't stick around for too long.

SHULKER

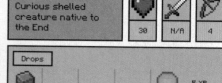

Curious shelled creature native to the End	♥	⚔	🏹
	30	N/A	4

Drops				
🐚			◯	5 XP

This shy little mob can be spotted in End cities, disguised among the native purpur blocks. It will stay hidden until a player is within range, when its shell will open and it will fire slow-moving projectiles that follow players. The projectiles cause a little damage, and makes players levitate!

Projectiles can be deflected back at a shulker with a weapon, or blocked by a shield, however. When its shell is closed, it has a hefty armour that will significantly reduce damage. When it gets hurt, it may try to teleport to safety.

HOW TO DEFEAT

It can be difficult to deal with shulkers in the narrow End towers that they normally reside in, especially if you're hit with Levitation. Make the towers inhospitable by plugging the doors and any gaps with blocks, then flooding with a lava bucket. This will cause them to teleport to an air empty space nearby – or if there isn't one available, they'll drown. If they have found a space, then bide your time, dodge their projectile attacks and line up a good crossbow shot.

SKELETON

Bow-wielding bony bane found all over the world			
	20	2.5	4

Drops

    5-8 XP

Be careful in dim areas, as skeletons are likely nearby. They always have a bow, and sometimes use tipped arrows. There's a chance that they'll be rocking some armour too. They circle around targets to avoid being hit, but won't try to evade any attacks.

HOW TO DEFEAT

Being comprised solely of bones has its pros and cons – skeletons can't drown, but they are irresistible to wolves. If you release tamed wolves, they'll chase skeletons away and attack them. Be sure to follow closely to save your loyal wolves though, as the skeletons will retaliate once they take damage.

SKELETON HORSE

Skeletal steed that arrives in a flash			
	15	N/A	N/A

Drops

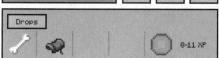 8-11 XP

There's a small chance that a lightning strike can summon a skeleton horse and rider. The humble skeleton now rides a bony steed and wields an enchanted bow! The horse is much faster than its bony rider, so it can be harder to hit, though it's slightly weaker too.

HOW TO DEFEAT

The easiest way to beat a skeleton rider is to get rid of the bony horse. Target the horse first, either with a bow or crossbow, to fell the rider and then take care of the skeleton alone. That way you won't have to deal with the greater movement speed or smarter defensive tactics of the equine undead.

SILVERFISH

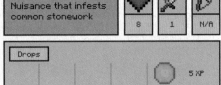

Nuisance that infests common stonework	♥	⚔	🏹
	8	1	N/A

Drops						
					⬡	5 XP

Be careful when mining blocks that seem like stone – sometimes they'll release silverfish into the wild. The silverfish itself is an annoyance like the endermite – it has a weak attack and very low health, though it can call in more silverfish to help out.

HOW TO DEFEAT

Beating the silverfish with a single blow is important – when it's wounded it will call allies to help it and you may get swarmed. The Bane of Arthropods enchantment will help out as with other insect mobs, but a netherite axe, diamond sword or a trident are all capable of ending a silverfish in a single blow anyway.

SLIME

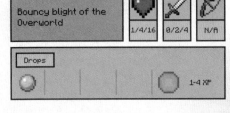

Bouncy blight of the Overworld	♥	⚔	🏹
	1/4/16	0/2/4	N/A

Drops				
⬡			⬡	1-4 XP

The slime is another mob that splits into smaller variants and attacks twice as fast as most mobs are able to. This gelatinous mob happily bounds around the Overworld until it spots a player. It will try to squish them by jumping on them, like magma cubes do.

HOW TO DEFEAT

Slimes can be overwhelming once they split into the smaller variants and you become increasingly outnumbered. Area-of-effect damage is the best way to deal with the horde – chuck splash or lingering Potions of Harming at the crowd to damage them all and you should whittle them down to slimeballs in no time.

SPIDER

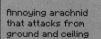

Annoying arachnid that attacks from ground and ceiling	16	2	N/A

Drops

   5 XP

The scuttling spider roams freely around the Overworld. If they're spotted in daylight, they remain passive to players unless they're attacked, but when the sun goes down, they'll become instantly hostile, even climbing sheer walls to get to their target!

HOW TO DEFEAT

Spiders are quick and agile, and they're not slowed down by cobwebs. The Bane of Arthropods enchantment can apply a high-level Slowness effect on spiders in addition to causing even more damage with each attack. A good axe enchanted with Bane of Arthropods will cleave through a spider in just a couple of strikes.

CAVE SPIDER

Eight-legged dweller of the underground	12	2	N/A

Drops

 5 XP

Not another one! The bluish hue of this arachnid sets it apart from its cousin, and it only spawns in mineshafts. Cave spiders are also passive in bright light, but otherwise aggressive. They can inflict Poison, which will reduce a target's health over a time.

HOW TO DEFEAT

You'll want to avoid their venomous bite so while Bane of Arthropods can be helpful, you won't want to get within melee distance. Instead, take your time and keep your distance, attacking with a crossbow. It has less health than a normal spider, so a few shots should be enough to put an end to this critter.

SPIDER JOCKEY

Nightmarish amalgamation of two sinister mobs	♥ 32/36	🗡 2	🏹 4

Drops

5 XP

Sometimes skeletons ride normal and cave spiders, though each have separate health and attacks. If it spawns in a snowy biome, there's a chance the rider will be a stray and in the Nether, it may be a Wither skeleton!

HOW TO DEFEAT

Divide and conquer! The spider is weakest, so try to take that out first. Keep your distance to avoid giving the jockey an easy target, then ready a crossbow, enchanted with Multishot or Piercing and take out the skeleton's steed. Now you can deal with the skeleton as you would any other bony beast.

STRAY

Frozen foes that can really slow you down	♥ 20	🗡 2	🏹 5

Drops

    5 XP

If the harsh climate of cold biomes wasn't hard enough, know that these icy skeletons are lurking there too. They're as dangerous as a normal skeleton with its bow, but strays also inflict Slowness, reducing movement speed and making it harder to escape.

HOW TO DEFEAT

If you're afflicted with Slowness, it might cause a problem if you can't catch the stray in order to defeat it. Tridents can be very useful here – enchanted with Riptide, it will propel you forward as you throw it – though only in wet conditions. Better yet, enchant it with Loyalty and the trident will return after each throw.

VINDICATOR

Axe-toting protectors of woodland mansions			
	24	13	N/A

Drops
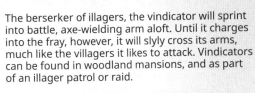 5-8 XP

The berserker of illagers, the vindicator will sprint into battle, axe-wielding arm aloft. Until it charges into the fray, however, it will slyly cross its arms, much like the villagers it likes to attack. Vindicators can be found in woodland mansions, and as part of an illager patrol or raid.

Their axe slashes are powerful and even more so if they have spawned with an enchanted axe! Be especially aware of any vindicators named Johnny – they're known to be hostile to all non-illager mobs and ghasts.

HOW TO DEFEAT

Their strong axe attack and the fact they often ride ravagers means that ranged attacks are the best tactic. Enchant a bow with a combo of Punch, Flame and Infinity to gain an endless supply of arrows that will simultaneously set the vindicator on fire AND keep it at a safe distance, where it can do you no harm.

WITCH

Horrifying hag with offensive concoctions aplenty			
	26	N/A	6

Drops

5 XP

If you go down to the swamp today, you're sure of a big surprise: a potion-launching witch! These mischievous magicians brew splash potions to throw at any adventurers that come near their huts. They can often be found wandering outside of swamps, spreading their misery around the world.

When defeated, they can be a valuable source of brewing ingredients, but when alive, they can inflict status effects such as Poison, Slowness, Weakness and Harming with their mystical concoctions.

HOW TO DEFEAT

The witch also packs healing potions, so the fight is best finished off quickly. Getting up close will cause the witch to use either splash Potions of Weakness or Harming, but go in with a good sword or axe enchanted with Sharpness and you should be able to defeat it before it can throw a second potion.

WITHER SKELETON

Charred, bony
residents of
the Nether

 20   8   N/A

Drops

     5-17 XP

At first glance, the Wither skeleton might just look like a dark, brooding cousin of its Overworld counterpart, with similar health and a basic sword.

However, this skeletal menace has a melee attack that's over twice as powerful! Not only that, but they inflict the Wither ailment on players, which gradually reduces health. Thankfully, they'll only spawn in Nether fortresses so you won't encounter them if you steer clear of those structures.

HOW TO DEFEAT

The Wither skeleton has immunities coming out of the holes where its ears used to be – fire, Poison and Wither statuses have no effect, nor does sunlight, drowning or lava. A sword strike though? That'll do! Enchant it with Smite to do extra damage against this undead mob, and block blows with a shield.

ZOMBIE

Common flesh-hungry hunters			
	20	3	N/A

Drops

     5-8 XP

If you hear a murmuring outside your base at night, chances are it's a zombie. They may even break down wooden doors and enter bases if they're smart. These undead mobs spawn regularly as the sun sets and seek shade when it rises, or they will burn away.

They call in backup from a wide area when they're attacked and can quickly become a difficult horde to contain. Individually, they're not too scary – they have average health and attack unarmed on most occasions, though they can pick up and equip weapons and armour!

HOW TO DEFEAT

Zombies shouldn't be much of a problem. You can sleep through the night – if they're not too close – wake up refreshed and let the sun do the rest. If they prevent you from sleeping, or hide in shade, throw splash Potions of Healing outside to drive them away and deter others from visiting you.

BABY ZOMBIE

Adorable, yet still vicious, undead creatures			
	20	3	N/A

Drops

      12 XP

Good things come in small packages ... and so do bad things. Not only does the baby zombie have identical health and attack to adults, but they're also much faster, making them more of a handful. Luckily, they also share weaknesses to healing and sunlight too.

HOW TO DEFEAT

Smaller zombie means a smaller target – add the increased speed, and this may be a difficult battle. Archers could take one out with a crossbow, but it's easier to go after it with a sword. Splash potions of Healing cause damage without accuracy, and a Potion of Swiftness will help you keep up with the little terror.

ZOMBIE VILLAGER

Innocent townsfolk fallen prey to the undead			
	20	3	N/A

Drops

          5-8 XP

When a village is overwhelmed by zombies, townsfolk may be turned into members of the legion themselves. Zombie villagers resemble villagers and even retain clothes they wore in a past life, though they have the tell-tale green skin of zombiekind.

HOW TO DEFEAT

All the normal undead tactics will work well against zombie villagers, but there is a non-violent means too – curing them! First you'll need to apply the Weakness effect by splash potion or tipped arrow. Once it has Weakness, you must feed it a golden apple and wait for the transformation to take place. Pacifism works too!

WITHER

Three-headed terror that only the foolish or the brave summon	❤️ 600	🗡️ 15	🏹 8

Drops

 | 50 XP

You've sharpened your steel against skeletons, creepers and zombies, but now it's time for the first of the boss mobs: the horrific Wither! This gigantic beast doesn't spawn naturally, so you must summon it only when you're ready for an epic challenge or you want to get your hands on a Nether star. Make sure you've got all your weapons primed and ready to go!

SUMMONING

Build a T-shape – like you would when summoning an iron golem – with soul sand or soul soil then place three Wither skeleton skulls on the top three blocks.

Once the third skull is in place, the creation will begin to grow, glow blue and remain invulnerable. Then it will do a massive explosion and begin actively attacking.

ATTACKS

The Wither's main attack is to shoot explosive skulls at you! The blue ones are slower than the black, but cause more destruction – though both do the same damage to a player. If you're hit by one, it will also inflict the Wither II effect on you, which depletes health over time.

When you've cleaved half the Wither's health, it will create another giant explosion and gain armour. It will also summon Wither skeletons to the fight and switch to a dash attack, where it charges at you and throws skulls. The dash is dangerous so make sure to keep a distance.

HOW TO DEFEAT

The Wither has a mammoth amount of health and immunities to fire, lava and drowning. However, it's undead so has a good amount of vulnerabilities, and it will also attack many other mobs, which will leave Wither roses behind to be wary of!

Build iron golems in various spots, which will distract the Wither, or damage it when it's close enough. As it flies around, your best option to attack it is with a ranged weapon – the crossbow could be particularly useful here if enchanted with Quick Charge and Multishot. Load with tipped arrows of Healing and you can make a huge dent in that health bar.

When the Wither starts to dash, have a Smite-enchanted sword at the ready to swipe at it while you dodge out of the way. Use a bucket of milk if you take a hit to get rid of the Wither effect before it can sow too much chaos. Have patience and stick to these steps and you'll be able to rid the world of the Wither after a well-fought victory.

ENDER DRAGON

Swooping draconic menace of the End

❤ 200	🗡 10	🏹 6

Drops

⬣ | ⬡ 12,000 XP

The final challenge, the one that every step of progress has been building to, is this: the Ender Dragon! This jet-black terror awaits you on the other side of an End portal, and will pose your fiercest and most puzzling challenge in the three dimensions. It doesn't have as much health as the Wither, but the process of battling the Ender Dragon is a lot more frustrating!

DRAGON HUNTER

Once you're through the End portal, you'll spawn on or near a small obsidian platform close to the central End island, where the gigantic winged beast will be circling, waiting for its next challenger. You'll also see a handful of large obsidian pillars, which are topped with End crystals that the dark dragon uses to heal itself when it gets injured in battle.

IDEAL LOADOUT

Before we jump into tactics to defeat the Ender Dragon, here's a recommended loadout that will negate some of its attacks and maximise your own damage potential.

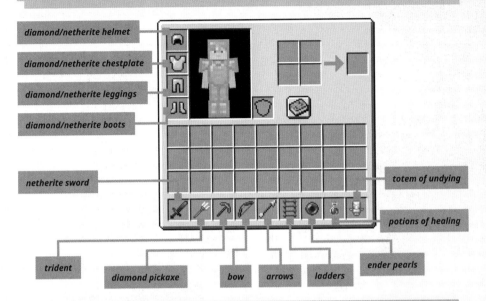

diamond/netherite helmet

diamond/netherite chestplate

diamond/netherite leggings

diamond/netherite boots

netherite sword

totem of undying

potions of healing

trident

diamond pickaxe

bow

arrows

ladders

ender pearls

ATTACKS

The Ender Dragon has three attacks to use against you.

If you destroy an End crystal, it will stop circling and swoop in to launch a fireball at you. These can't be deflected and instead cause a lingering cloud of damage around the impact site.

Sometimes the dragon will stop for a rest on one of the exit portal structures surrounding the island, and from its perch will unleash its dragon breath attack, which is a thick cloud of purple smog that damages any mob within it.

Finally, and most dangerously, the dragon can divebomb you with a powerful melee attack, which flings you up to heights that would kill you if you drop. The attack does twice as much damage if the dragon's head hits you compared to the rest of its body.

HEALING PREVENTION

Not only is the Ender Dragon a dangerous foe, it's also a very clever one. The End crystals that sit atop the obsidian pillars will automatically heal the Ender Dragon when it's close. You should destroy as many as possible before attacking the dragon, otherwise your offensive efforts will be futile.

When you destroy a crystal, it will cause a damaging explosion – including to the Ender Dragon if it's healing – so it's best to attack it from a safe distance. This might not always be possible to begin with as some are protected by cages that need to be mined away. Use ladders or Ender pearls to reach the iron bars, destroy them with a pickaxe then get back to ground to attack the crystal.

HOW TO DEFEAT

The Ender Dragon is immune to all status effects, and flies rapidly around the island. Attacking with a bow is difficult due to the dragon's speed, but it is possible. It will take four times as much damage on its head than any other part of the body, so aim just in front of its trajectory to maximise your damage potential.

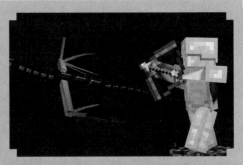

When the dragon is perched, it won't take damage from arrows, so switch to a trident enchanted with Loyalty and keep throwing until the dragon flies off. If it swoops in, slash with a netherite sword. You're likely to take some damage and possibly be flipped into the air too. Fling Ender pearls at the ground to land safely, then restore any lost health before it can attack again.

DROPS

If this is the first time that you've vanquished the Ender Dragon, you'll receive a whopping 12,000 xp reward! Just look at all those orbs! Two types of portals will also open up – one of them will take players back to the Overworld, while the End gateway will lead to the eerie outer islands of the End.

Atop the exit portal, you'll see the real prize – a dragon egg. It's a trophy that proves you've defeated Minecraft's most magnificent mob. Of course, it's not so simple to collect this either, as it teleports every time you try to mine it. Instead, use a piston to push the dragon egg and it will drop itself as an item, ready to take pride of place in your trophy cabinet.

ROUND 2?

Was one battle not enough? Some players like to keep their skills sharp by challenging the dragon repeatedly. It's also the only way to obtain dragon's breath, which is used to brew lingering potions.

To summon the Ender Dragon again, you need to place 4 End crystals around the exit portal, which will deactivate and reset the battleground for a rematch. Players will only receive 500 xp when they defeat the dragon after the initial fight.

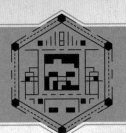

MOB ALLIES

FOX

20   2

Gain the trust of a fox by feeding it sweet berries and you'll have a cute ally at your side. A loyal fox will follow a player around and can be leashed too. It will attack most hostile mobs that attack a trusted player by pouncing at them.

HORSE

15-30   0

Utilitarian beasts that can carry you into battle or speed up travel. You must continually mount a horse and avoid being bucked off in order to tame it. You can equip a saddle and horse armour on a tame horse to get it ready for battle.

IRON GOLEM

100   21.5

Calling an iron golem an ally is a stretch – it's more like a mob-obliterating hero that you summon. They can be made using 4 blocks of iron and a carved pumpkin. They will attack most hostile and neutral mobs, except creepers and wolves.

LLAMA

15-30   1

The llama is a walking, spitting storage unit. Tamed llamas can be equipped with a chest and led with a lead so you always have resources to hand. Other llamas dwelling nearby may also follow a tamed llama to make a caravan.

Not every mob you encounter will be out to get you. There are some, in fact, that can help you, whether you're charging into combat on their back, carrying your overflowing inventory or backing you up in battle. Let's meet some of the friendlier mobs that can aid you.

CAT

10   3

Cats rarely take to humans as much as humans take to them, but if they happen to be lolling around you, they will deter the advances of creepers and phantoms! Just keep them away from chickens and rabbits!

SNOW GOLEM

4   0

You can create a snow golem with two stacked blocks of snow and a carved pumpkin on top. They'll throw snowballs at nearby mobs, even if they aren't hostile. Their snowballs only cause knockback, though they will damage a blaze.

STRIDER

20   0

It's nice to see a friendly – if unhappy – face in the Nether. Striders can't be tamed, but they can be saddled and ridden, even across lakes of lava. You'll need a warped fungus on a stick to control its movements though.

WOLF

20   4

Wolves exist in the wild wooded taiga biomes and can be hostile if attacked. However, feed a wolf a few bones to tame them and give them a nice, red collar. When tamed, you can give wolves commands and they'll attack mobs you're attacking!

VERSUS MODE

You've sharpened your blade against the mobs of
the Overworld, the End and the Nether, but your biggest
challenge still awaits ... defeating other players. Read on
to discover tactics for facing off in PvP battles, different
playstyles to even the odds, and how to build an arena in
which to prove you're the real champ!

THE GREATEST CHALLENGE

WHAT IS PVP?

PvP stands for 'Player Versus Player' and refers to any game mode where you challenge a real human rather than the game's AI (sometimes known as PvE: 'Player Versus Environment'). PvP doesn't change Minecraft at all – you'll still swing swords and shoot arrows – it just means you're competing with other players!

DO I HAVE TO FIGHT MY FRIENDS?

You can if you want, but you can create multiplayer modes that don't rely on combat. Some are assault course races, or elytra tracks that challenge people to swoop around a track, while others might challenge your accuracy at an archery course. There are dozens of modes to play, so try a few and see what you like.

IT'S ME AGAINST THE WORLD?

Not necessarily – it depends which mode you choose. You can adapt most to become team games. Instead of going 1v1 in a battle, you could make teams of three instead. Or maybe your assault course is a relay, where a team's times are added to see which total is fastest.

Not even the greatest programmer can give mobs an AI to match the wits of a human (not yet anyway), which is why many flock to PvP in search of a greater challenge. If you're ready to swap collaboration for competition, then read on to take your first step into the world of PvP.

COUNT ME IN! HOW DO I JOIN A PVP GAME?

A very good question – the most important thing to note is that you can set up a PvP game in ANY world. To make it PvP, you just need other people! You have multiple options to set up or join a multiplayer game and we'll cover some of the simpler ones for Bedrock Edition on the next pages. For more options, visit **help.minecraft.net**

SETTING UP A GAME

YOUR WORLD, YOUR RULES

Whenever you create a world, you'll be given a set of options that let you alter the type of world that generates. You can also edit the Settings on your existing world by pressing the edit icon next to any world. Let's look at a few of the options you can use to change how you and your friends interact with your world.

GAME MODE

Choose between Creative, Survival and Adventure; Creative is best for building battlegrounds. Change to Survival or Adventure – which stops you breaking certain elements – when you're battling.

PLAYER PERMISSION WHEN JOINING FROM INVITE

This controls how much other players can interact with a world. The best one for PvP is 'member', which lets players break blocks and battle mobs or players.

FRIENDLY FIRE

Finally, the good stuff! This toggle will determine whether players can cause damage to each other in your world. Turn this on when battle commences!

MOB SPAWNING

Unless mobs are relevant to the game you're trying to create, you don't need them around. Flicking this toggle will prevent them from spawning.

Once you've got your world ready and all your buddies are here to test their mettle against one another, you might wonder how you turn that world into a PvP arena. Here are a few quick tips to make sure you're beginning the battle on the front foot.

WHO WANTS TO PLAY?

If you navigate to the Multiplayer part of the Settings menu, there are a few more things you'll need to make sure you do. The first one is to make sure that the multiplayer toggle is on, otherwise nobody can join your world!

Secondly, you'll want to change the Microsoft Account Settings option to be either 'Friends Only' – which means only people who you're friends with on a chosen system can join – or 'Friends of Friends', so your buddies can bring along someone not on your friends list.

PVP GAME CREATIONS

ARENA

Your basic PvP game mode is a straight-up battle. Grab a weapon, don some armour and try to deplete your opponent's health bar before they do the same to you! You can shake up the formula by inviting more friends, buddying up to create teams, or deciding to have a limited inventory to give players a uniquely different style of play (see page 90 for more on this).

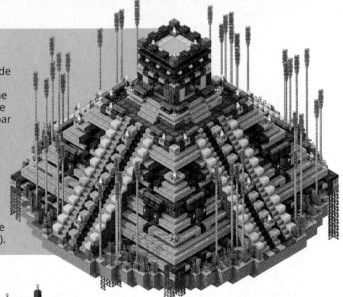

SPLEEF

In spleef, the aim of the game is to be the last player to fall through various levels of destructible blocks. You don't necessarily need to fight each other in this mode as you'll more often than not be aiming for the blocks below opponents' feet to make them drop down to the next level. You can make the floors from blocks like wool to make them easier to destroy with a single hit.

Finally, it's time to talk about the different types of PvP game you can set up in your world. Whether you fancy some one-on-one combat, a team brawl or you prefer a test of speed or intelligence instead, there's something here for everyone.

ELYTRA RACE

Take to the skies with nothing but a pair of elytra on your back and fireworks in your hand in a race to the finish line. You'll be weaving in all directions to pass through hoops that mark the route of the race, using the fireworks to blast you in different directions at speeds mere landlubbers can only dream of.

RAIL SHOOTER

If you're not so good with heights, then racing on rails might suit you more. This minigame involves riding in minecarts around a track, but with an additional layer – targets! They're dotted along the track to test accuracy while moving and the winner is the first to activate all their targets. It's a white-knuckle ride!

SKY WARS

With a bit more of a focus on building and tactics, Sky Wars is a game mode intended for the more patient PvPer. Each player or team starts off on a floating island with limited resources, and must craft and build their way to other islands to battle opponents and claim resources for themselves. Or they could lie in wait and spring a trap ...

COMPETITIVE TACTICS

PREP WELL

If you step into an arena with a bunch of other players, you can be sure they're fully armoured and armed to the teeth, so make sure you go into battle equally prepared. There's nothing worse than starting a PvP match only to realise you're wearing a leather tunic and carrying only a wooden sword.

JUST LIKE YOU

You might be used to dealing with creepers and zombies, where the mobs' actions are predictable, but the opposite is true in PvP. Your opponent will move erratically, do things that don't make sense and attack relentlessly. The good news is that you can do the same!

COMMUNICATION

You're probably used to playing with pals if you share a world with friends, so you might already be a teamwork pro. However, PvP is often much more frantic than building cool structures with your buddies, so make sure to communicate quickly and effectively to keep everyone on the same page during a bout.

We know that you've swung a sword and hefted an axe before, but is there a part of you that's just a little bit worried about the world of PvP. There's nothing to fear — except that trident flying towards you — but maybe a few final pro tips will have you starting out on the front foot.

CRITICAL TACTICS

If you're using a melee weapon, you can do critical damage by jumping while you strike, dealing 150% more base damage than a normal blow. You need to be falling from your jump to land a critical hit, rather than ascending, but if you can master this, it's deadly!

INDIRECT ATTACKS

If you're playing in an expansive area, or on a team of players, you might be able to set up some traps that can protect you from behind or lure players in. Digging a trench behind a block-high wall could trap players for you to pick off from range, while dispensers can be loaded with all manner of projectile to protect narrow routes.

KNOW WHEN TO RUN

There's no shame in trying to escape if things aren't going your way. Running away could mean the difference between winning and losing. Smart warriors will take time to hide, heal and come up with a new plan of attack before re-entering the fray. Knowing when to escape is as important as attacking and defending.

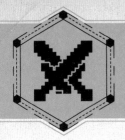

THE ARENA

THE ARCHIPELAGO

At the four corners of The Arena lie the islands of The Archipelago, the floating bases of a Sky Wars battle.

GLADIATOR PIT

Surrounded by spectators, the sandy pit is where warriors fight to the death in armed combat.

Now you're fully prepared for any PvP situation, you need somewhere to stage your competitions, and what better place than The Arena, a multi-faceted stadium that has everything you need to host races and battles for your friends.

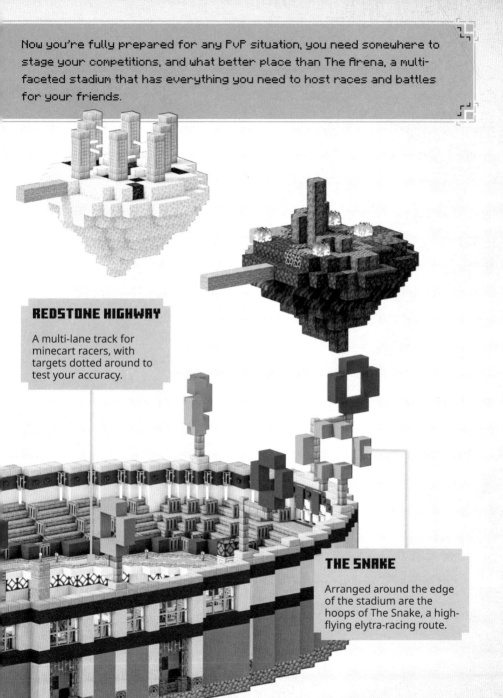

REDSTONE HIGHWAY

A multi-lane track for minecart racers, with targets dotted around to test your accuracy.

THE SNAKE

Arranged around the edge of the stadium are the hoops of The Snake, a high-flying elytra-racing route.

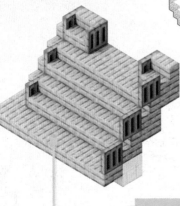

STRUCTURE

The Arena has a common oval track base, which allows a nice open space for combat in the centre.

SEATING

The wooden tiers are made from stair blocks, with some premium seating available with trapdoor arms.

ENTRANCE

The lofty elytra launch pad overlooks the hidden entrances where warriors enter the arena.

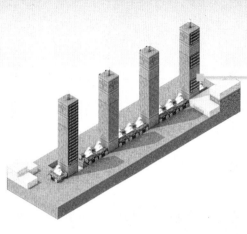

VERTICALITY

Agile competitors might be able to climb aboard the combat towers and make use of the height advantage. But what goes up must come down.

READY ROOM

The ready room, nestled underneath the seats, allows players to choose equipment before entering.

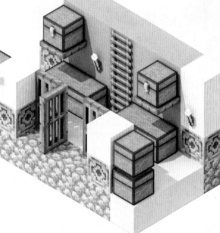

HOLDING GATE

These partitions stop any competitor getting a head-start, and can even hold a mob surprise ...

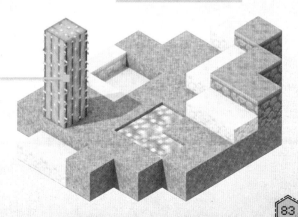

HAZARDS

The floor of The Arena is littered with damaging hazards to watch out for during battles.

TRACK LAYOUT

Following the curve of The Arena, the Redstone Highway is made from a mixture of rails and redstone torches

DUAL TRACKS

The parallel tracks are different lengths, so the outer track has more powered rails to compensate and ensure speed equality.

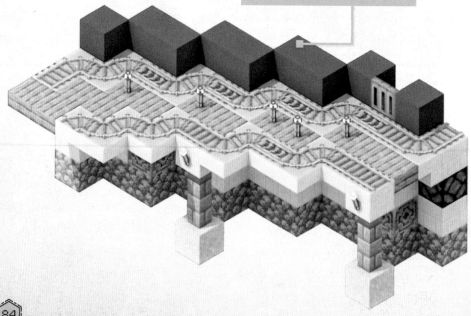

LIGHT 'EM UP

Hitting a target block will send a charge to the redstone lamp to signal that a player has hit the target. The first person to hit all their targets and light up all their lamps wins.

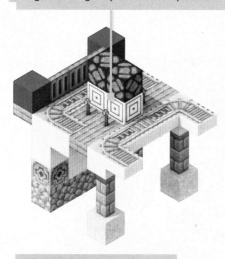

READY FOR TAKE-OFF

Elytra-clad racers will start their race through The Snake from this elevated platform, which will allow them to gain some gravity-assisted speed.

PUT A RING ON IT

The rings surrounding The Arena have 2x2 holes in them, making them very tricky to pass through at speed. They're also at different elevations, making it anything but a smooth flight.

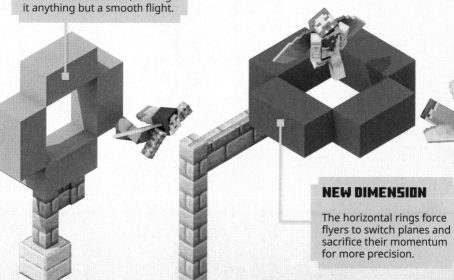

NEW DIMENSION

The horizontal rings force flyers to switch planes and sacrifice their momentum for more precision.

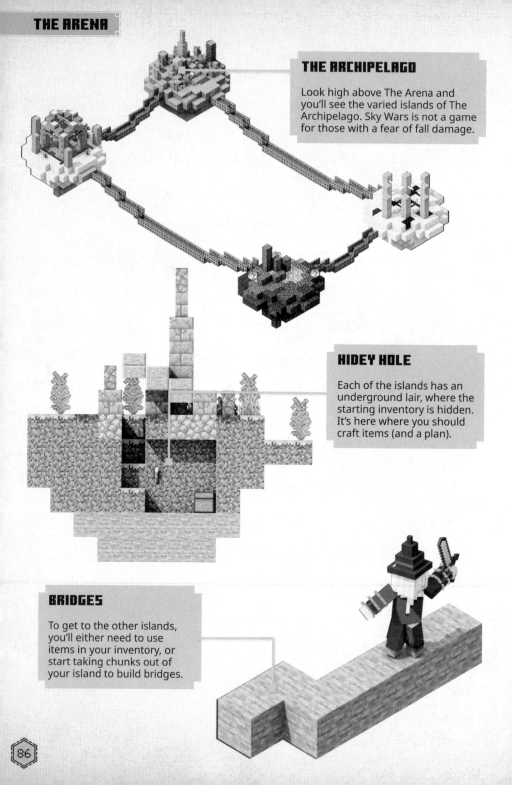

THE ARCHIPELAGO

Look high above The Arena and you'll see the varied islands of The Archipelago. Sky Wars is not a game for those with a fear of fall damage.

HIDEY HOLE

Each of the islands has an underground lair, where the starting inventory is hidden. It's here where you should craft items (and a plan).

BRIDGES

To get to the other islands, you'll either need to use items in your inventory, or start taking chunks out of your island to build bridges.

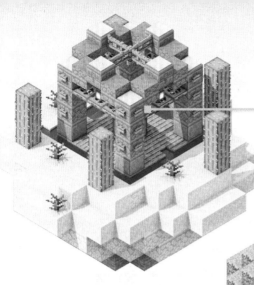

DESERT ISLAND

With suffocating sand and spiky cacti to hand, the desert island could well be the perfect place to spring a trap.

SKY GARDEN

This idyllic paradise has plenty of easily mined blocks, which could help you make headway to other islands.

NETHER LAND

This island has blocks that can easily harm players, so everyone will need to keep their wits about them when they arrive.

THE END POINT

Though there aren't that many useful blocks here, at least there's plenty of obsidian to hunker down behind.

CHOOSE YOUR FIGHTER

NEW WAYS TO PLAY

You might think that you're at a disadvantage by only having a certain number of blocks and items at your disposal, but that's the point – everyone is. If you're all limited to certain weapons and armours, it puts everyone on a level playing field and encourages you to come up with strategies that you otherwise might not have.

HOW DO I ADD LOADOUTS?

You can easily set this up in Creative mode – before switching out again for battle of course – just grab the items you see for any particular class from the Creative inventory and place them in a special 'class chest'. Then each player will choose one of the chests at random to select their class. If you want to be extra-clever, you could even put the outfit on an armour stand too.

TOP TIP

Experiment! You don't have to stick with the classes on these pages. Play around with different loadouts to create your own versions to use in battle. Just make sure to keep the fight fair and make all your proposed loadouts balanced.

Do you find yourself spamming the same tactics over and over? Have you grown weary of wielding your trusty axe in every PvP battle? Why not freshen up your skills by adopting a 'class' – a distinct loadout and equipment that encourages you to play in a completely new and exciting way!

ELEMENTOR

HOTBAR

With the power of the elements at her fingertips, the Elementor class has the forces of the land behind her. Her channelling-enchanted trident can call in lightning, she can summon frosty snow golem to aid her in battle, and her mastery of snow (and shovels) can lay traps that enemies will never suspect. Oh, and she can breathe underwater.

VALKYRIE

HOTBAR

					Potion of Slow Falling	Potion of Strength	Potion of Leaping	Lingering Potion of Weakness

Is it a bird? Is it a plane? Nope, it's a war-forged Valkyrie swooping down for a brawl. She brandishes a sword enchanted with fire aspect, which will set enemies ablaze, before she assembles a launch pad out of a piston and slime block to fling her back up into the skies to seek out her next target. She also has some back-up weapons in case she fancies a different form of melee.

DIVINER

Sent from the heavens to aid the more modest combatants, the diviner is a perfect support class. His tipped arrows can boost friends on the battlefield, and his infinity-enchanted bow is blessed to never consume his limited stash of arrows. Of course, his totem of undying will give him more than one chance if the battle doesn't go his way.

HOTBAR

Arrow	Arrow of Healing	Arrow of Regeneration	Arrow of Leaping	Arrow of Strength		Potion of Regeneration	

PYROMANCER

HOTBAR

Potion of Fire
Resistance

This dragon-headed warrior may look scary ... because he is. He has plenty of explosive surprises up his sleeve, able to set up manual fireball launchers using dispensers, levers and fire charges, or lay a world-obliterating trap with TNT and pressure plates. If you get close enough to be struck by his netherite sword, consider yourself one of the lucky ones.

ALCHEMIST

HOTBAR

Lingering Potion of Poison	Lingering Potion of Weakness	Splash Potion of Slowness	Splash Potion of Decay	Potion of the Turtle Master

Time spent tinkering with metals, enchantments and potions is time well spent indeed. The Alchemist knows this better than anyone, having used his sorcery to create his golden armour and axe from basic stones. He likes to take a back-seat on the battlefield, lobbing potions of all manner at friend and foe alike, and letting his arbitrary arsenal of potions sow seeds of chaos.

GOODBYE

Hey, look at you! You've become a seasoned warrior, with fire in your eyes. We hope you'll stride out across the Overworld with new confidence, or enter the arena with your mind set on fabulous victories.

What you've learned through the pages of this book goes further than just fighting. Maybe you've also learned new ways to brew, or set your eyes on enchanting which will take you on new adventures. Perhaps you've even added a new appreciation for ghasts? And of course, you've learned a lot about combat.

As with any new skill, you'll need to keep practising to fully develop into the fighter you can be. But don't forget that you're bound to find yourself defeated along the way. Probably many times! Remember that no warrior ever earned their stripes without getting a few bumps and scratches in return. The important thing is to get back up again and have another go!

Right, it's time to stop dilly-dallying. Take up your sword, strap on your chestpiece, and ...

HAVE AT YOU!

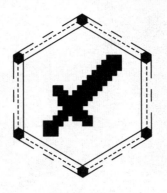